Contents

Introduction 4

Lawns, Flowerbeds, Fruit
and Vegetable Plots 6

Trees, Shrubs and Hedges 50

Ponds 100

Wild Areas, Compost Heaps
and Log Piles 122

Above and Below 138

Introduction

It's official: the UK has a lot of gardens. At the last count we had over sixteen million of them! We tend to think about our gardens (like our houses) as our own private property, but, whether we like it or not, we share our gardens with masses of wildlife.

You might think that your garden is pretty small. Maybe you have a patch of grass, a few flowers or shrubs, perhaps a tree. How can it be a rich **habitat** for wildlife? The reason is that your garden isn't an 'island'. Robins and hedgehogs don't see next-door's garden as off-limits. In fact, they might see the hedge between numbers 10 and 11 as a wildlife corridor, a nesting spot or a place to **hibernate**, not just a boundary between properties.

Think of your garden as a patch of material. When you join it to all the neighbouring gardens, it becomes the most enormous patchwork quilt! In fact, if you think about all the gardens in the country added together, they suddenly become the biggest nature reserve in Britain.

Many of us like our 'patch' to look as attractive as possible, so we plant flowers, shrubs and trees. You might have a pond to help you relax, a lawn to play on, or maybe you grow fruit and vegetables. By making your garden a beautiful, relaxing and fruitful place, you can also turn it into a haven for wildlife: part woodland, part meadow, part wetland and part quiet corner.

To the creatures we share them with, our gardens are giant stores of food. Over 99% of the wildlife in your garden doesn't have fur or feathers, though. Even the most empty looking garden contains thousands of different types of insects, spiders, woodlice, and slugs. You might not notice them but these small creatures are really important as they provide food for the showstoppers: **mammals**, birds, **reptiles** and **amphibians**.

As well as loving our gardens, many Brits are also big nature lovers. Close to half of us have fed garden birds and many of us spend a small fortune on a whole variety of plants, shrubs and trees. Turning your garden into somewhere that wildlife would like to spend time in, doesn't have to cost a lot of money and can be surprisingly easy.

This book will help you to recognise most of the wildlife that has flown, crawled, jumped, or dug its way into your garden. It will also give you top tips on how to make your garden even better for wildlife. Remember, if you have a garden then you have your own nature reserve on your doorstep - and it's up to you to enjoy it!

Lawns, Flowerbeds, Fruit and Vegetable Plots

For creatures that walk, crawl or fly, the green, green grass of home is much more than just a garden lawn. To a hedgehog, bumblebee or butterfly, your back garden is a rolling grassland or wildflower meadow.

Flower-rich meadows have mostly been lost from the British countryside. Building and modern farming methods mean that 97% of our traditional meadows have simply disappeared. This means that gardens with lots of flowers are now important **sanctuaries** for a whole range of wildlife, struggling to find a home in the countryside.

Many of the creatures that eat plants, or search for **nectar** or **pollen**, look on your flowerbeds as a rich meadow. And, wherever there are insects feeding from our flowers and birds eating seeds, there will also be **predators**, keen to make a meal out of the unwary. The lawn, flowerbeds and vegetable plot might seem peaceful to us humans but for wildlife it's a 'dog-eat-dog' world!

Follow me to see who lives here!

FOX

The fabulous Mr Fox first moved into London after World War II, having been only an occasional visitor before. He has since found living alongside us so appealing, that there is barely a town or city across the land that doesn't provide a home for the only wild British member of the dog family.

Rubbish bags. . . yum!

Foxes eat more or less anything: birds they catch on the lawn, rats they snatch from the vegetable bed or beetles they find in the flowerbeds. They find plenty of rich pickings in our gardens. Even if there is no live **prey** to pounce on, foxes are perfectly happy to polish off spilt bird food or to raid any rubbish bags left out for collection.

Making a home

Many gardens have a shed or a patch of bushes and shrubs which can be the perfect place for foxes to have a family. Foxes dig holes in the ground, called 'earths', to live in. The foxes' strong smell and mess, close to the entrance of their earth, mean you can often tell a fox family has moved in well before you see their babies, or cubs, in spring.

Come out to play

After their first few trips above ground, the chocolate-brown cubs quickly gain confidence. They spend their first few weeks exploring every corner of their home patch. The playful cubs might trample flowers or chew your gardening gloves but if you are lucky enough to see one of our largest **mammals** from your doorstep it will be a thrill.

Hedgehog

Recently voted the nation's favourite animal, the hedgehog finds an important sanctuary in our gardens. As Britain's only spiny **mammal**, you won't mistake one for anything else! Hedgehogs are secretive and shy so they are more common in gardens than many people think, although their numbers have gone down recently.

Watch out slugs!

Hedgehogs usually come out under the cover of darkness and lawns or flowerbeds make the perfect hunting ground for their favourite foods — worms and slugs! Hedgehogs track down their food using their excellent sense of smell and sensitive whiskers. As well as worms and slugs, hedgehogs also eat insect **larvae**, beetles and even birds' eggs if they are lucky enough to find them. Gardens often have bushes, hedges, compost bins or log piles where hedgehogs can hide during the day and **hibernate** in winter.

Everybody loves me!

Who loves me?

Danger

The hedgehog's only natural **predator** is the badger, which uses its strong paws to bypass the hedgehog's defences and open it up like a tin can. In gardens where badgers are common hedgehogs are often thin on the ground. However, badgers aren't to blame for the recent decline in hedgehog numbers. Two of the main reasons for this seem to be the hedgehog's poor road sense as curling into a protective spiny ball isn't much protection against a car or lorry, and loss of good garden habitat.

Rabbit

Rabbits were first brought to Britain from the Mediterranean by the Normans nearly 1,000 years ago for their meat and fur. Today, there is hardly a corner of Britain that is 'bunny-free'. Rabbits are most at home in the countryside but it's no surprise that some bunnies have been tempted into rural gardens for a cheeky nibble!

Rabbit or hare?

With their long, pointy ears, large eyes on either side of their heads and white underside to their tails, the only animal the rabbit could be confused with is the larger brown hare. Unlike rabbits, which spend much of their time underground in holes called 'warrens', hares spend their whole lives above ground. Hares also stick more to farmers' fields and so you won't often see one in a garden. They are larger than rabbits, have longer, black-tipped ears and are able to run much faster.

Rabbit

Hare

I can spot the difference!

Eat and be eaten

If it's green, then there's a good chance a rabbit will eat it! Rabbits sometimes annoy gardeners by nibbling away at anything from the lush grass of the lawn to prized flowers and vegetables. Rabbits themselves are the food of a wide variety of animals such as foxes and buzzards. The presence of people scares off all but the boldest **predators** though, so rabbits do find **sanctuary** in gardens.

The Thrush Family

You can see three different members of the thrush family in gardens all year round. These woodland birds have realised that lawns and flower borders are often full of worms, slugs and snails during the summer and berries during the winter.

Blackbird

- the male has black feathers
- yellow beak
- eye rings
- makes a 'tchook-tchook-tchook', alarm call

Male blackbirds like to charge around the lawn searching for earthworms and bossing other birds about.

Mistle Thrush

- bigger than a song thrush
- grey-brown back
- spotted chest and sides
- nests in woodland

You are most likely to see a mistle thrush in your garden in spring or summer months, looking for beetles, earthworms, slugs and snails.

Song Thrush

- smaller than a blackbird
- warm brown upper parts
- black spots
- pale breast
- excellent hearing and eyesight

DID YOU KNOW?

Song thrushes like eating worms but in dry weather they can be hard to find, so the clever thrushes switch to eating snails instead. A thrush holds a snail in its beak and then uses a rock to smash the snail's shell open and get at the juicy contents inside.

More Lawn-Loving Birds

Starling

Despite a worrying decline in numbers, the starling is still a common bird across the country. There are very few gardens that won't have been visited by at least a small flock of them. From a distance, starlings might look dull and boring, but if you are lucky enough to get a close up view you will see they are anything but! In the **mating season** a male's feathers have an oily purple, violet and green sheen, which makes them dazzle when the sun is out.

Garden helpers

Starlings are happy to take handouts from your bird table, which they might dominate by turning up in a gang. The good news for gardeners is that starlings are just as happy finding food on your lawn. By digging up insects' **larvae**, like leatherjackets and cockchafer **larvae** which munch on grass roots, starlings help gardeners produce healthy green grass.

Pied Wagtail

The pied wagtail is a common sight across the UK and an exciting entry on the list of wildlife you might see in your garden. These busy little birds can sometimes be spotted on the lawn, where they half walk and half run around, on the hunt for flies, midges, caterpillars and spiders.

As their name suggests, wagtails waggle their tails up and down all the time! Why they do this is a bit of a mystery; one theory is that it helps them scare any hiding insects out into the open so that they can catch and eat them.

Those wagtails just can't stop wagging their tails!

Butterflies

A Butterfly's Life

Butterflies lay eggs which hatch into caterpillars.

Caterpillars eat lots of leaves until they have had enough, then they turn into a chrysalis.

The adult butterfly comes out of the chrysalis.

Butterflies drink nectar.

Butterflies

large black **eyespot**

orange on
the forewings

Meadow Brown

The **eyespot** makes the butterfly
seem larger and more scary to
frighten **predators**.

Ringlet

The ringlet likes the shady parts
of the garden in high summer.

eyespots or 'ringlets'

chocolate brown wings

Common Blue

You might see a male common
blue in your garden looking for
nectar and females.

males have lilac-blue wings

females have blue
and brown wings

19

Butterflies

in the Flowerbeds

Peacock

Peacocks' wings are nearly black underneath to help them to hide from hungry birds.

When to look for them: any sunny day from early spring to early winter.

large **eyespots**

Small Tortoiseshell

Small tortoiseshells like to sit with their wings open to the sun.

When to look for them: any warm day

checked orange and black markings

Red Admiral

Most red admirals can't survive the cold winters in Britain so if you see one in your garden it could have flown all the way from central Europe.

When to look for them: summer

Orange-Tip

If you see a male orange-tip butterfly patrolling the flower borders in the search for females it is a sign that spring has finally sprung!

orange tip on wings

mossy green pattern underneath

Comma

Commas were once rare, but they have spread in recent years and can now be seen as far north as Scotland.

When to look for them: look out for commas eating blackberries or other fruit in the autumn.

ragged, torn-looking outline

white, comma-shaped mark

DID YOU KNOW?

The comma gets its name from the white comma-shaped mark on the underside of its wings, which is only visible when its wings are closed.

Green-Veined White

Green-veined whites are often mistaken for one of the 'cabbage whites', whose caterpillars eat your cabbages. However, green-veined whites actually like to lay their eggs on plants like cuckooflower and garlic mustard.

green wash of scales

21

Butterflies

Known together as the 'cabbage whites', these two types of butterfly can make gardeners tear their hair out! If you don't manage to keep the egg-laying females away from the vegetable plot early in the year, then the caterpillars that hatch out will eat all your cabbages.

Large White

Females find cabbages or Brussels sprouts by smell, and then lay up to 100 eggs on the leaves.

When the caterpillars hatch, they swarm all over a plant, eating as much as they can and growing quickly.

black wing tips

black spots

grey wing tips

Small White

As you might have guessed, a small white is smaller than a large white! In a good year, a small white can have up to three different **generations**, so they can attack your cabbages from mid-March right through to the first frosts of autumn.

Moths

Most moths are only active at night, so they would be difficult to see if it weren't for the fact that a lot of them are attracted to light. If you are interested in moths you could use a moth trap. Moth traps use a bright light which attracts moths from around the garden. It has a large entrance hole but a small exit so the moths can't escape until you have had a look in the morning.

Garden Carpet Moth

- the patterns on the wings look like patterned carpet

The patterns help the moths to **camouflage** themselves when they rest during the day.

When to look for them: between April and October.

long proboscis for drinking nectar

Hummingbird Hawk-moth

- the only British hawk-moth to fly during the day

Hummingbird hawk-moths fly here all the way from southern Europe.

When to look for them: warm summers

Here's a hummingbird. Can you see how the hummingbird hawk-moth got its name?

Garden tiger caterpillars are often called 'woolly bears' because they are very hairy. Look out for them sitting in the sunshine.

Garden Tiger

- look for the bright colours and crazy pattern

Garden tigers are tricky to spot because they only come out at night.

Elephant Hawk-moth

- pink and lime green coloured wings and body

Elephant hawk-moths are active after sunset and the adult moths feed from lots of different garden flowers.

When to look for them: between May and early August.

DID YOU KNOW?

The elephant hawk-moth gets its name from its **caterpillar**, which looks a bit like an elephant's trunk!

This is an ermine or stoat. Can you see how the white ermine moth got its name?

White Ermine

- white wings with black dots
- striped black and yellow body warns **predators** the moth doesn't taste nice

The white ermine enjoys many plants that you might have in your garden, including nettles and docks.

When to look for them: mid-May to late July.

Heart and Dart

- look for the heart-shaped and dart-shaped markings

Heart and dart caterpillars hide in the soil in the daytime and come out to feed at night.

When to look for them: at dusk between May and August.

Large Yellow Underwing

- one of the most common moths to see flying against lit windows in summer

- bright yellow **hind** wings

After dark, the large yellow underwing visits many of your garden's **nectar**-rich plants for a quick feed. The females lay their eggs in large batches on your plants.

When to look for them: between June and October, but most common in August.

Silver Y

- one of the most common moths to see flying during the day

- silver 'y' shaped marks on wings

Most of the silver Ys you see in your garden will have flown here from mainland Europe. Silver Y caterpillars feed on lots of different plants but don't often live through our cold winters.

White Plume Moth

- pure white in colour
- wings split into feathery plumes

White plume moth caterpillars feed on bindweed, which is a very unpopular weed with many gardeners.

When to look for them: June and July.

DID YOU KNOW?

White plume moths and mother of pearls are both micro-moths. This means that they tend to be smaller than most other moths and are simple in design.

Mother of Pearl

- looks washed-out
- greenish-purple tinge to wings

The mother of pearl is one of many insects whose caterpillars feed on nettles. When they are not feeding they also hide in the rolled-up leaves for protection.

Bumblebees

A big, furry queen bumblebee, which has just woken up from **hibernation**, brightens up any sunny spring day. Once awake, the queen's first job is to fill herself up with **nectar** before searching for a hole to make her nest in.

White-Tailed Bumblebee

One of the first bumblebees to wake up is the queen white-tailed bumblebee. They are a common visitor to gardens, as they busily work their way around a whole range of flowers. They only have short tongues so the **nectar** in long-necked flowers is out of their reach. But, not to be defeated, they can 'steal' the **nectar** by 'drilling' a hole at the base of these flowers!

yellow stripes on the **thorax**

yellow stripes on the **abdomen**

white tip

Buff-Tailed Bumblebee

Queen buff-tailed bumblebees have similar yellow bands to white-tailed bumblebees but, as their name suggests, they have a buff (pale brown) tip to their **abdomen** instead. Like their white-tailed cousins, they also make a habit of stealing **nectar** from flowers. Their large underground nests can contain over 300 worker bees!

Red-Tailed Bumblebee

Red-tailed bumblebees are out and about searching for a nesting place from March onwards. However, they have to watch out because sometimes their nests are taken over by the similar looking cuckoo bumblebee, later in the spring. A queen cuckoo bumblebee kills the queen red-tailed bumblebee and then forces the red-tailed bumblebee workers to care for the cuckoo bumblebee **larvae**!

red tip to the abdomen

Common Carder Bee

Common carder bees get their name from their habit of combing (or 'carding') moss and dried grass to make a more comfortable nest. These bumblebees have long tongues and you might spot them disappearing into foxglove flowers to collect the **nectar** right at the bottom of the tube. Common carder bees make quite small nests, with rarely more than 100 worker bees.

ginger and black

29

Wasps and Honeybees

Both wasps and honeybees are very sociable insects and always live in large groups. They are both yellow and black, which warns other animals to 'leave well alone'. If you ignore the warning you might get a painful sting. However, that's where the similarities between wasps and honeybees end.

Common and German Wasps

Found in most gardens, these two different wasps look very similar to each other. Both common and German wasp queens wake up in the spring and start to make a nest. They chew up wood scraped from dead trees or garden fences and mix it with their spit to make a kind of paper. They then use this to make a round nest, either underground, in an attic, or in shrubs and trees.

Inside the nest, the queen lays eggs which hatch to become the first workers. This all-female workforce keep adding to the nest and feeding the new **larvae**. These worker wasps feed on **nectar** and, if you have ever been to a barbecue or picnic, you will know that they like fruit and sugary drinks. However, the new **larvae** grow very quickly on a different diet. They feed on chewed-up insects which are collected from around the garden by their older sisters. In this way, wasps provide a pest removal service, which helps keep your garden in the best possible condition!

DID YOU KNOW?

Wasps can sting as many times as they like but bees have a barb on their sting. This means they can only get you once and will die afterwards.

Hornet

The hornet is the largest of all the wasps and packs a powerful punch if provoked! They often nest in hollow trees. Their **larvae** are fed by around 900 workers on a diet of flies and other insects from around the garden. Later in the summer, as the workers start to die, the new queens hatch and then **mate** with male hornets before they **hibernate**.

Eeeek! We'd better try not to annoy her...

Honeybee

If you spot honeybees in your garden, it probably means that within a few kilometres of your house someone is keeping bees. People first started keeping honeybees thousands of years ago and beehives can contain more than 50,000 worker bees surrounding a single queen. Honeybees are experts at finding food and they collect **nectar** and **pollen** from lots of different flowers, to feed themselves and the **larvae** back at the beehive. Honeybees are important insects in gardens and the countryside because they **pollinate** many fruit trees, vegetables and crops.

Solitary Bees

Not all bees are sociable like the honeybee. Many types of bee are happiest on their own; these bees are known as solitary bees.

Tawny Mining Bee

Tiny mounds of soil in your lawn can mean only one thing – your garden is home to mining bees! The tawny mining bee is one of the most common mining bees in Britain. The reddish-coloured female bees dig tunnels and then lay a small number of eggs in them. They also leave behind a paste of **nectar** and **pollen** so that the hungry **larvae** have something to eat when they hatch.

Patchwork Leaf-Cutter Bee

If you find semi-circles cut out of the leaves of your roses, you probably have patchwork leaf-cutter bees in your garden. The female bee cuts off pieces of leaf and then rolls them up to carry them back to her nest tunnel. She uses them to line her nest and also to act as 'doors' between her different **larvae**. When her eggs hatch, the **larvae** feed on this, before breaking out through the doors as adult insects.

Red Mason Bee

Red mason bees are important because they **pollinate** many of your garden plants. The female bee collects **pollen** in a little basket below her **abdomen**, which she then brings back to a hole in an old wall or tree stump. She lays around 10 eggs in each tunnel and leaves a mixture of **pollen** and **nectar** behind for the **larvae** to eat when they hatch. The tunnels are then sealed with mud, which the female bee presses down using special horns on her head.

Bugs

reflective wings

Common Flower Bug

The common flower bug eats greenfly and spider mites, both of which are garden pests, so flower bugs are insects that any gardener should be happy to welcome. You can tell you've found a common flower bug by its reflective wings and the black plate which covers a large part of the bug's **thorax**.

black plate on thorax

Greenfly

Greenfly aren't really flies, but they are really green! Greenfly are actually sap-sucking aphids and are probably public enemy number one for gardeners all over the world. Greenfly are often found on roses. They use their sucking mouthparts to tap into plants' sugar-rich juices. When there is plenty of food, aphids can multiply in number incredibly quickly.

Common Froghopper

The **nymphs** of this bug produce 'cuckoo spit'. Look out for it on grasses or other plants in spring. The **nymphs** create the 'spit' by mixing air with a **substance** they make in their bodies and it helps them to hide from **predators**. Adult froghoppers are one of the champion jumpers in the animal kingdom. They are able to use their spring-loaded legs to leap up to 70 centimetres!

Ladybirds and Beetles

Seven-Spot Ladybird

Seven-spot ladybirds have three black spots on each wing case and a seventh spot which is shared equally between the two wing cases. Females lay batches of little yellow eggs on any plant where their favourite food, greenfly, live. The six-legged ladybird **larvae** look nothing like the adults but both **larvae** and adults are greenfly-eating machines! As greenfly are pests for gardeners, this means that ladybirds are definitely a gardener's friends. They work hard to keep your plants in top condition!

DID YOU KNOW?

Ladybirds are actually a type of beetle! These colourful creatures are important **predators** of many pesky garden pests.

Two-Spot Ladybird

Two-spot ladybirds have a single black spot on each red wing case. They eat aphids for breakfast, lunch and dinner! The adult ladybirds often **hibernate** together and you can sometimes find large groups in sheds or underneath tree bark.

Lily Beetle

This beetle can be very annoying to gardeners who like to grow lilies. In spring, the bright red females lay lots of eggs on lily leaves and stalks. When the **larvae** hatch, they protect themselves from **predators** by covering themselves in their own slimy poo! Meanwhile, if you try to pick up an adult beetle they make a squeaking sound. Both the **larvae** and the adults eat lilies and can seriously damage your lily plants.

Violet Ground Beetle

With its purple sheen, the violet ground beetle is a lean, mean garden **predator**. They hide under logs or dead leaves by day and come out to hunt at night. They are quick on their feet and are able to chase down slower insects. The females lay their eggs in the soil and, when they hatch, the **larvae** are **predators**, too.

Slugs and Snails

Many gardeners hate slugs and snails as they love to eat garden plants, but they also help gardeners by breaking down all kinds of rotting leaves and dead animals. Slugs and snails are a useful food source for the birds, **amphibians** and **mammals** we love to see in our gardens.

Garden Slug

The garden slug is small, dark-grey, has a black line running along each side and is orangey-yellow underneath. This slug loves to eat your plants and attacks from both above and below. It likes the leaves of lettuces and also strawberries, while it goes underground to eat potatoes, carrots and beetroot!

Large Black Slug

The large black slug is one of the most commonly spotted slugs. They produce sticky goo which helps them to glide around, leaving a silvery trail in your garden. If you disturb this slug it will curl into a hump. They like to eat rotting plants, poo and dead animals!

Brown-Lipped Banded Snail

Most of the brown-lipped banded snails you will see in your garden have black and yellow bands (or stripes) on their shells. Look out for other colours though – you'll also see plain yellow, plain brown or even pink! Whatever colour the rest of their shell is, you'll always be able to tell it is a brown-lipped banded snail by the brown lip (or edge) at the shell opening.

Field Slug

Field slugs only grow to five centimetres in length. They have a short ridge, or 'keel', running along their backs from the tail end and are mostly a pale grey colour. Field slugs hide under leaves and stones in the daytime, then come out at night to munch your plants!

Garden Snail

You can often find garden snails clustered together under upturned plant pots. Their shells are brown with patterns of dark lines or blotches. They love to feast on the plants in your garden: both in the vegetable plot and flowerbed!

Spiders and Harvestmen

You'll see lots of these eight-legged **predators** in any garden with plenty of plants. There are over 600 different species of spider in Britain and a lot of those are regular visitors to gardens.

Garden Spider

Look out for the spiral webs of garden spiders on shrubs, fences or walls. Female garden spiders are much larger than the males and you can spot them by the pattern of white dots and ovals which make a small cross on their **abdomen**. Garden spiders trap insects with the tiny sticky droplets on their webs. They then quickly **paralyse** the insects they have caught with **venom** and wrap them up in silk to eat later!

Flower Crab Spider

Instead of using a web to catch her dinner, the female flower crab spider uses **camouflage**. She can change colour from white to yellow or light green, depending where she has decided to hunt. Once in position, she stays totally still, with her two long pairs of front legs raised and spread. If a hoverfly or bee comes too close, she grabs it!

Zebra Spider

The zebra spider doesn't use a web either – instead it uses its amazing eyesight, speed and jumping ability to catch its **prey**. The zebra spider's back legs give it the power to leap onto its **prey**, while it uses its front legs to grab its victim. This spider prefers warm weather, so you'll see this stripy **predator basking** in the sunshine, on walls and fences, during spring and summer.

Harvestman

Unsurprisingly, you'll find most harvestmen in your garden in autumn, around harvest time! Harvestmen have much longer legs and a smaller, more rounded body than spiders and they catch their **prey** without silk or **venom**. Their second pair of legs is longest and they use them to feel for **prey**. Once they have found their target they snatch it up with a small pair of pincers on their head and suck it dry!

45

Earwigs and Lacewings

common Earwig

You can easily recognise an earwig by its pincers. It is not always the most popular insect with gardeners as it has a habit of nibbling petals and tender leaves. They hide under logs and stones during the day as they are most active at night. Even though common earwigs are able to fly, you are more likely to see them scuttling around.

Female earwigs lay their eggs in the spring, after sleeping all winter in the soil. Unlike other insects, earwigs are careful mothers. Female earwigs look after their eggs, guarding them from **predators** and cleaning them to make sure they stay healthy. When the **nymphs** hatch out, they look like miniature versions of their parents and their mother cares for them until they are old enough to leave the nest.

Green Lacewing

The green lacewing has a pale green body and large transparent wings. They are definitely good friends to gardeners. Both the adults and **larvae** love to fill up on aphids and can play a big part in looking after your roses! Green lacewings **hibernate** in winter. When they wake up in the spring, the females lay up to 500 eggs, either singly or in batches on plant stalks. The eggs hatch out into shaggy-looking caterpillars which are after just one thing – greenfly!

DID YOU KNOW?

Lacewing **larvae** are a favourite food of birds such as blue tits, but they have a clever way of staying hidden. Once the **larva** has sucked an aphid dry, it sticks the remains to spines on its back as **camouflage.**

Welcoming Wildlife

Top Tips

1 Persuade your parents to leave a small section of the lawn un-mown to see what springs up. Plants such as daisies, self-heal, dandelions and different grasses will then have chance to grow. This lush **habitat** provides the perfect hunting ground for hedgehogs and is a good place for moths and butterflies to lay their eggs.

2 Try to grow lots of different flowering plants so that there is always something in flower. From the first warm days of spring to the frosts in autumn, there are insects buzzing around, desperate for the **nectar** and **pollen** they find in flowers.

3 Choose plants that are rich in **pollen** and **nectar**. These wildlife-friendly plants are sometimes marked with a bee logo in garden centres.

4 Don't use slug pellets. The pellets are hard to break down and can end up poisoning birds which eat slugs, like blackbirds and thrushes. Beer traps, crushed egg-shells and copper bands are all environmentally friendly ways to keep slugs away from your plants.

5 Don't worry about your plants being nibbled! Leaf-eating insects are vital to the wildlife in your garden and without them you would have fewer spiders, beetles, birds, **mammals, amphibians** and **reptiles**.

Wildlife-Friendly Plants

Ten great flowerbed plants

- Cranesbill
- Foxglove
- Hellebore
- Common valerian
- Lavender
- Lungwort
- Sage
- Thyme
- Wallflower
- Verbena

Five great lawn weeds

- Clover
- Daisy
- Dandelion
- Self-heal
- Yarrow

Five great fruit and veg plants

- Redcurrant, whitecurrant or blackcurrant
- Raspberry
- Broad bean
- Cabbage
- Runner bean

Don't forget I can help get rid of slugs too!

Trees, Shrubs and Hedges

Woodlands are one of the richest wildlife **habitats** in the whole of Britain. If you have space for trees and smaller shrubs in your garden it will give it an extra dimension – turning it from a bungalow to a block of flats!

The amount of food that trees and shrubs provide for wildlife is huge. Whether it is the millions of leaves, flowers, fruits and nuts you find in woodland or the actual wood itself, there is something to suit every taste. A single oak tree is able to support thousands of different insects, caterpillars and spiders. All those small creatures then, in turn, provide food for woodland birds and **mammals**.

The cracks in or behind tree bark and holes in tree trunks also give shelter to many animals. Some creatures live in these nooks and crannies for their entire lives, while others use them as safe places to bring up their young. The bark of a tree is also home to moss and **lichen**, while the tree's **canopy** acts as a walkway for squirrels.

The ground below trees and shrubs (the 'woodland floor') is another important **habitat** for wildlife. The flowers, which bloom before the trees' leaves have unfurled, provide **nectar** and **pollen**, which are vital for many insects when they wake up from **hibernation**. When the leaves on the trees do open, they create the shady conditions which some creatures need.

Let's see who lives here!

51

Badger

The badger only sticks its nose above ground as dusk approaches so it is no surprise that you don't see them very often. Their black and white face markings make the badger one of our most easily recognised and well-loved animals.

The family home

Badgers like company and often stick together in family groups of between five and ten animals. Badgers spend a large part of their lives underground in a sett, which they often build in or close to woodland. The sett is a network of tunnels and sleeping rooms, often on several levels. Badgers dig their setts using their powerful front paws and claws and many setts have been home to generations of badgers. The badgers constantly work on their homes: digging extensions, opening new entrances and even giving them a regular spring clean!

Juicy worms!

Badgers eat anything, from fruit and beetles to dead animals and leftover dog food, but their favourite food has to be earthworms. The worms in your lawn and flowerbeds make your garden an attractive place for badgers! Badgers track worms with their incredible sense of smell, which is 800 times more sensitive than a human's. Once it finds a worm, the badger uses its strong paws and claws to dig out a juicy meal, sometimes making a mess of your garden in the process.

Squirrels

Of the two squirrels seen in British gardens, the American grey squirrel is now the more common. You are only likely to see red squirrels in more remote parts of Britain. In fact, the grey squirrel has settled in so well in Britain that it is probably the wild **mammal** you are most likely to see in your garden.

Grey Squirrel

Grey squirrels were brought over from the forests of the United States of America around 130 years ago and have not looked back since. They have spread across Britain, and live very comfortably in parks and gardens. In fact, grey squirrels can live happily just about anywhere; all they really need is a few trees so they can scamper to safety if they sense danger.

Cheeky!

Some people don't like grey squirrels because they strip the bark from trees and have passed on a nasty disease to Britain's **native** red squirrels. But it would take a pretty hard-hearted person not to be secretly delighted by the grey squirrel's cheeky behaviour. As they run along the washing lines, leap from tree to tree and fill their cheeks with food from your bird table, the grey squirrel is one of the most entertaining wild visitors you'll meet!

Stop stealing my dinner!

Red Squirrel

Red squirrels were once found in most areas of Britain, but these days you would be very lucky to have our **native** red squirrel as a regular visitor to your garden. Aggressive grey squirrels have pushed out red squirrels and many reds have died from an illness picked up from the American invaders. Sadly, the only places where red squirrels now live happily are those areas that grey squirrels have yet to reach.

Smaller than their American cousins, red squirrels are ginger in colour and have tufts of hair on their ears. They now live in Scottish forests and a few places in England, Wales and Northern Ireland. If you are lucky enough to have them in your area, you could try putting out food on a bird table to encourage these shy creatures out of the trees and into your garden.

Deer

Deer have no natural **predators** to keep their numbers down in Britain and so sightings of deer in gardens are becoming much more common. They are tempted in by the rich pickings on offer in many gardens. There are two different types of deer that you might see and they come from very different parts of the world.

Roe Deer

The beautiful and elegant roe deer is the smallest of all the native deer. They are most active at dawn and dusk and the males (or bucks) can be easily recognised by their short antlers. The males use these to fight for females (or does) and also to defend their **territory** from other bucks in the summer. Roe deer **mate** in the summer but the does don't have their babies until the following spring.

Tasty leaves!

Roe deer like to eat tasty leaves so it is no surprise that they have been tempted into many **rural** gardens. They usually visit when you are in bed so look out for nibbled plants, the footprints of their hooves and a generous sprinkling of their shiny, black droppings!

Yum!

Muntjac

Muntjac were introduced from Asia into a large estate in Bedfordshire just over 100 years ago. It was not long before they escaped! They have found Britain to be a perfect adopted home and have spread across southern England, reached mid-Wales and are currently moving towards Scotland.

Flower munchers

People are amazed at how small muntjac are – barely bigger than a medium-sized family dog. Their success is partly down to their unfussy diet – if it's green, they'll eat it! They can also produce young at almost any time of the year which means that they can quickly multiply their numbers. Like the roe deer, muntjac are busiest at dawn and dusk and are sometimes unpopular with gardeners as they will munch on your prized flowers!

Watch out – they'll eat anything green!

Mice

Hi!

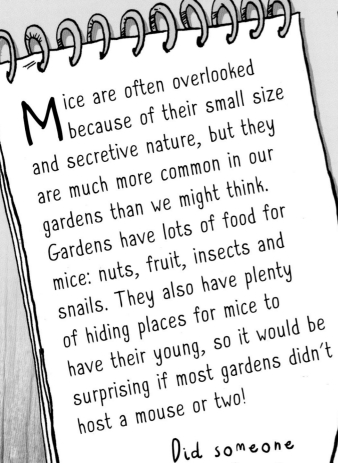

Mice are often overlooked because of their small size and secretive nature, but they are much more common in our gardens than we might think. Gardens have lots of food for mice: nuts, fruit, insects and snails. They also have plenty of hiding places for mice to have their young, so it would be surprising if most gardens didn't host a mouse or two!

Did someone say food?

Wood Mouse

You can spot a wood mouse by its warm-brown coat, large ears, bright eyes and long tail. They might well be the most common type of **mammal** in Britain. A single female can have up to 20 young between spring and autumn and their numbers probably reach over one hundred million by the end of the summer. Wood mice hop and bound along on their large back feet and come out at night to avoid hungry **predators**.

Yellow-Necked Mouse

Yellow-necked mice are similar to wood mice, but they are only found in the southern half of England and Wales. They are slightly larger than wood mice. As their name suggests, they have a yellow band in between their front paws and across their necks, which makes them look as though they need a wash! The yellow-necked mouse is happiest in old, **mature** woodlands but many also come into gardens in winter.

House Mouse

The house mouse was accidentally introduced from Asia over 2,000 years ago. These days, they don't just live in our nice warm houses! During the summer months, our gardens are just as attractive to this adaptable and tough little animal. House mice are smaller and greyer than our **native** British mice and you can often tell that house mice are around by their strong, mousey smell. House mouse numbers have gone down recently as we leave less food and rubbish around for them to eat, but where there is good bed and breakfast on offer, this mouse is still common.

63

Birds

Busiest during daylight hours, birds are often the most obvious wild visitors to your garden. Thanks to the food we leave out, many of the birds that are normally found in woodlands can now be seen in gardens.

Robin

Robins are one of Britain's best-known and favourite birds. The robin, with its red **breast**, is associated with Christmas. Robins often defend their **territory** – or your garden – all year round, not just during the **breeding season**. This means robins are one of the few birds that can be heard singing on Christmas day!

Gardener's friends

Robins are known as the 'gardener's friend', because of their habit of following anyone digging the soil so that they can snatch any earthworms or juicy morsels which are uncovered. In autumn and winter, robins switch from their summer food, which is mostly insects, spiders and caterpillars, to fruits and berries.

Eeek! I'm outta here!

Wren

With over eight and a half million pairs, the wren is the most common bird in the UK. You can spot a wren by its small dumpy body, narrow, upward-pointing tail and busy nature. Wrens can look more like mice than birds as they scuttle around your garden, looking for beetles, spiders, flies and caterpillars.

Nest builder

Despite its tiny size, the male wren has a powerful, rattling song. The male builds the domed nest out of leaves, grass and moss, but leaves his mate to line it with feathers and hairs that she has collected.

Dunnock

Often called the hedge sparrow, the dunnock is not actually a sparrow at all. This brown and grey bird is often seen creeping around on the ground, nervously flicking its wings. Dunnocks stick close to the edge of woodland, so any similar areas in your garden offer the perfect place for them to find food and raise their young.

Family life

When it comes to looks, the dunnock is not the most striking bird in the world but, while it may be a bit dull-looking, it has an interesting family life. Some **broods** are raised by a male and a female, while others are raised by a male and two females or one female and two males.

House Sparrow

House sparrows live happily alongside humans but there has been a worrying drop in their numbers over the last 30 years. Despite this decline they are still a common sight in gardens across the UK. Male sparrows have a grey patch on the top of their heads and black on their throats, but the streaky brown females stand out less.

Mess is best!

Sparrows like to nest in the roofs of houses and you can often tell where they are by listening out for the chirping call of the males. The adults mostly eat nuts and seeds but their young chicks like a diet of insects, and caterpillars. Scientists aren't sure why house sparrow numbers have declined so much, but the research suggests that they prefer messier gardens!

Goldcrest

Weighing no more than a 20 pence coin, the goldcrest is the UK's smallest bird. You can spot the females by the bright yellow patch on their heads. The males have an orange patch as well as a yellow one. Goldcrests are always on the move as they hunt down insects, spiders and caterpillars. They prefer to live in **conifers**, and the fact that these trees are popular in gardens is one reason why goldcrests might pay you a visit, even in the depths of winter.

Pigeons and Doves

Woodpigeon

With over five million pairs in the UK, there can be very few gardens that haven't been visited by the greedy woodpigeon. Look out for them finishing off any spilt seed from your bird feeder or bird table. They don't just eat bird food, though; they also eat fruit, buds and even cabbages. Woodpigeons are able to **breed** right through spring and summer and can have up to three **broods** a year.

- bulging chest
- white neck patch
- white crescent on their wings in flight

Feral Pigeon

Feral or town pigeons are the **descendants** of wild rock doves, which can still be seen in remote parts of Scotland today. They have swapped the cliffs and ledges of their original homes for the man-made versions in our towns and cities. Pigeons are experts at finding food and many of them visit **urban** gardens to see what they can find to eat. They are often dismissed as 'flying rats' but the streetwise feral pigeon is a bird with a fascinating life and so is deserving of our respect.

- smaller than woodpigeons
- colour varies from pure white to almost black

Collared Dove

Before 1955, the collared dove didn't **breed** in the UK, but, since then, their numbers have grown to close to a million pairs. They are very happy to live alongside humans: around farms feeding on spilt grain or in gardens with bird tables. Their repetitive 'coo-cooo-cuk' call is a familiar garden sound in the spring and summer.

- small in size
- long, white-tipped tail
- pinky-brown and grey colour
- thin black bar on the side of the neck

listen out for the noise they make!

69

Birds of Prey

If you have woodland birds feeding and nesting in your garden, you might also see **birds of prey**, which specialise in eating those birds!

Sparrowhawk

Normally a **predator** of small woodland birds, the sparrowhawk has realised that hunting around bird feeders can be an easy way to catch lunch! With over 35,000 pairs in Britain, sparrowhawks are now the commonest **bird of prey** in gardens. Using speed, skilful flying and great eyesight, they are the ultimate flying hunters!

Sneaky tactics

Sparrowhawks use surprise to catch their **prey**. They try to stay out of sight until they reach top speed, only coming into view at the last moment so that the feeding birds have no time to escape. The males are smaller which means they can chase down birds like great tits and greenfinches. The larger females hunt bigger, meatier birds like blackbirds, starlings and even pigeons.

Eek!

Phew! Glad I've got my prickly coat!

Tawny Owl

Tawny owls are usually tucked quietly out of sight up a tree during the day, only coming out at night. They are quite noisy birds, so you are more likely to hear than see one! Of the five types of owl which are seen regularly in the UK, the tawny owl is the one happiest in towns, and is a surprisingly common visitor to many gardens with large trees.

WATCH OUT!

They are well **camouflaged**, with rich-brown feathers streaked with darker and lighter browns. In the countryside, tawny owls mostly catch small **mammals**, but in gardens they often hunt birds. Starlings, sparrows and blackbirds, as well as the odd squirrel or rat, regularly turn up on their menu. Tawny owls nest very early in the year and are very aggressive when defending their nest and chicks: human **intruders** beware!

Woodpeckers

Great Spotted Woodpecker

The great spotted woodpecker is by far the most common of the three British types of woodpecker and is often seen swooping down to bird feeders, scattering the smaller birds. Great spotted woodpeckers are mainly black and white. They also have deep red underneath their tails and some red on their heads, which varies depending on their age and sex. In fact, the only bird you might mistake them for is the much smaller and rarer lesser spotted woodpecker.

Long tongues!

These woodpeckers very rarely spend any time on the ground and are happiest up in the trees. You might hear their loud call of 'kick', or the drumming sound made by the males in early spring, which they use to attract the local females. They use their beaks to dig out beetles and their **larvae** from their tunnels in trees. They have long tongues, which they use to snatch up any insects that are too difficult to get at just by digging.

Green Woodpecker

The green woodpecker is sometimes known as the 'yaffle' because of its loud, laughing call. They are the largest and most brightly coloured of all our woodpeckers. Adult green woodpeckers have a crimson-red coloured 'cap', a greenish-grey upper body and a bright yellow bottom, which shows up like a light bulb during the woodpecker's bouncing flight!

Ants, ants, ants!

Unlike the great spotted woodpecker, the green woodpecker spends a lot of time on the ground, moving around in a series of jerky hops. It particularly likes gardens where there are ants' nests. When it finds a nest, the green woodpecker uses its long tongue to get at the yummy eggs, larvae and ants inside! Despite being happy on the ground, green woodpeckers still need large trees to **breed** in, bringing up their chicks on a rich diet of... ants!

The Crow Family

Magpie

Like all members of the crow family, the magpie is shy of humans but becomes much bolder when tracking down food. They are known for raiding other birds' nests to eat the eggs or chicks and for catching and killing small **mammals**; the magpie is definitely one of the garden's top **predators**. Some gardeners don't like magpies for this reason but there is no **scientific evidence** that they cause the numbers of other garden birds to drop.

blue-green sheen on dark feathers

pinkish body colour

Jay

Jays can be difficult to spot when they are quietly perched in a tree. Often it is their harsh screech-like call which can give you a clue to where they are. Like the magpie, the jay eats the eggs and chicks of other birds, as well as fruits, seeds and acorns. When there is a lot of food around, jays like to bury some but they often forget where they have left it. This means that they may well have planted many of the oak trees around Britain!

white bottom

blue flash on the wings

Jackdaw

The jackdaw is the smallest member of the crow family and they have realised that chimneys are not that different from the holes in trees in which they used to nest. They often eat the food we leave out for smaller birds, arriving in gangs to scoff the lot before you are even out of bed! The jackdaw is the most common of all the crows in Britain and most of their success is down to their ability to find food both in trees and on the ground. They eat almost anything and everything!

ash grey 'hood'

pale eyes

DID YOU KNOW?

The jackdaw's name comes from its loud call of 'tchack'!

75

Tree Experts

Nuthatch

Nuthatches use their tree-climbing skills to track down spiders and beetles in the summer, or to look for seeds and nuts in the winter. Nuthatches are so good at climbing trees that they are the only British birds which are able to climb down a tree head first. They look a bit like small, big-headed woodpeckers, with a blue-grey back and head, whitish tummy and chestnut sides. A black line runs straight through the nuthatch's eyes, making it look a bit like a mini-bandit!

Home birds

The best way to find a nuthatch is to listen for its loud call of 'tuit, tuit, tuit!'. They don't often move far from their homes but if your garden is close to woods and you have bird feeders up, you have a good chance of encouraging nuthatches to leave the safety of the trees.

Treecreeper

Looking more like a mouse than a bird, the treecreeper does exactly as its name suggests; it creeps up trees! It uses its long, downward-curving beak to pick out spiders, beetles and caterpillars from the tree's nooks and crannies. Using its long, stiff, tail feathers to support itself against the bark, this bird was made for a life in the trees.

The only way is up!

Treecreepers only ever climb up trees. They start at the bottom, moving up in a spiral to cover as much of the trunk as possible. As they approach the top, treecreepers search the smallest branches and only fly down to the bottom of the next tree when they can creep no higher!

Winter Visitors

You might think it is cold in winter but, compared to some countries, our winters are warm! Birds from those countries are regular visitors to our gardens in the winter as they come here to escape the cold and to eat the fruit from our shrubs and trees.

Redwing

Redwings are related to our **native** thrushes. They cross the North Sea each autumn, flying all the way from Scandinavia and Iceland. They mostly travel at night and make a distinctive 'see-ip' call as they fly.

pale eyebrows

rusty-red sides

spotty breast

Passing through

Shy birds by nature, redwings travel around the countryside in small flocks and don't settle anywhere for very long. If your garden has lots of trees and bushes dripping with berries you might find that redwings come to visit you. In winter there could be as many as 700,000 redwings here but, by April, they will all have flown back North to **breed**.

grey head

chestnut back
and wings

spotty
breast

grey bottom

Fieldfare

Fieldfares are another member of the thrush family which comes to visit. They like company, spending time with other fieldfares and also redwings. You might be able to hear the 'chacker, chack, chack' call they make. You can spot them between October and April, feeding on berries. You might also see them if you have an apple tree in your garden as they love eating the fallen fruit.

Waxwing

Waxwings are quite a sight in winter. Their raised **crest** and bright colours make them look like miniature 'pink punks'! The numbers visiting Britain each winter vary a lot. Some winters bring just a handful of birds, while in other years thousands come. Arriving in northeast Britain, flocks then spread across the country, stripping fruit as they go. They can eat two or three times their own body weight in berries every day!

pink crest

black throat

The Tit Family

Blue Tit

Many blue tits nest in gardens. Natural nest holes can be hard to find so they are often happy with nest boxes instead. Blue tits can have up to 10 chicks and a **brood** of hungry babies can eat over 10,000 caterpillars in between when they hatch and when they finally leave the nest.

blue 'cap', wings and tail

black 'eyeliner'

yellow belly

black 'cap', collar and throat

white cheek patches

Great Tit

The great tit is the biggest of the tit family. It uses its size to push smaller birds away from bird feeders when it visits. Listen out for their call of 'teacher-teacher' in spring. Great tit chicks eat caterpillars and usually only take three weeks after hatching before they learn to fly. They are often still fed by their parents for a bit longer, however.

yellow breast

black stripe

Coal Tit

The coal tit is the smallest and most timid of the tits that might visit your garden bird feeder. They only dash in to grab a seed when there are no other birds around and then fly straight back to a quiet corner to eat! Being small can be useful. Coal tits can hang upside down on the small branches or even hover like hummingbirds to reach caterpillars.

white stripe on the back of the head

small and light

small, round body

Long-Tailed Tit

Long-tailed tits aren't really related to the other members of the tit family. They are very friendly and are most often seen in family groups of up to 20. They particularly like fat balls because they provide lots of energy to get them through the winter. On the coldest nights, families of long-tailed tits huddle together to share warmth.

long, narrow tail

pink, grey, black and white feathers

Finches

Chaffinch

The chaffinch is only beaten by the wren when it comes to the honour of being our most common bird. There are over six million pairs in the UK. The males have a blue-grey hood and pinkish **breast,** but the females are much duller in colour.

Clearing up

Chaffinches can live anywhere with some trees and shrubs. Like many small birds, they eat caterpillars and insects in the spring and summer and then seeds in the winter. Look out for them on the ground below bird feeders, clearing up the food that other birds have dropped.

Greenfinch

During the winter, greenfinches are quite common in **rural** gardens. They come in gangs and use their size to get the best food. The males are mossy green in colour with yellow flashes on their wings and tails, whilst the females are much less showy.

cosy nests

Greenfinches sometimes **breed** in gardens. Their well-hidden nests are made out of twigs and moss before being lined with something softer, like hair or wool. Out of the **breeding season**, greenfinches often mix with other finches to feed on seeds and the stubble from farmers' fields. Food in the countryside is becoming harder for finches to find, as farmers use new methods, so gardens provide an important source of winter food.

Goldfinch

Easily our prettiest finch, the goldfinch's red, white and black face is just as striking as the gold flashes on its wings. A group of goldfinches is called a 'charm' and it is easy to see why!

Roller coaster nest!

Thanks to an increase in the number of us feeding the birds in our gardens, goldfinches are now seen in twice the number of gardens as they were 10 years ago. They use their beaks like a pair of tweezers to get the seeds from plants such as thistles and teasels. Goldfinches **breed** in gardens as well as the countryside. They hide their nests well, in the outer branches of trees and bushes. That means on a windy day, being in the nest must be like riding on a roller coaster!

Bullfinch

The striking bullfinch is a shy but surprisingly common visitor to many **rural** gardens. Similar in size to a sparrow, the chunky bullfinch never gets too far from safety. They quietly fly out to feed, before disappearing back into the trees. With his black cap, beautiful rose-pink **breast** and white bottom, the male is a very smart bird. The females aren't as colourful, though.

Food, glorious food!

Bullfinches like to eat the tender flowers and buds of fruit trees in the spring. They like the sunflower hearts people leave on their bird tables, and in the autumn they eat seeds and fruit from trees and bushes. The bullfinch's short, strong beak is very powerful and is perfect for cracking seeds to get to the tasty contents inside.

Winter Finches

Winter is the best time for spotting woodland birds in your garden and, if you look carefully, there might be some rarer visitors among the more common tits and finches.

Siskin

In the winter, you might see siskins among the more common finches in your garden. They look like greenfinches, although they are a bit smaller and more brightly coloured. Like most British finches, the males are far more striking than the females. With his black cap, yellow flash on his wings and forked tail, the male siskin is an exciting visitor to see in your garden.

Local knowledge

They like to feed in alder and birch trees, delicately teasing out any small, tasty seeds. If you see a siskin it is unlikely to be alone. They travel in flocks and use their local knowledge to keep track of trees coming into seed. They also top up their diets with the free handouts they can get from bird feeders. They **breed** in Wales, Scotland and in continental Europe so most siskins in southern England will have moved on by April.

Brambling

Bramblings are similar in size to their cousins the chaffinches. It is quite rare to see them in British gardens. They **breed** in Scandinavia and Russia and in some years large numbers spend the winter in Britain, feeding on beech seeds and the spilt food below bird feeders. In other years, however, only a few cross the North Sea to Britain.

In summer, the males are a stunning combination of orange, black and white. Unfortunately, we rarely see them at their best, as in winter they look like they've faded in the wash!

Summer Visitors

L ook out for these two visitors in your garden. They come here because of the insects in the summer and the berries in the autumn.

Chiffchaff

In the summer, the chiffchaff comes to Britain from Spain or even Africa. The easiest way to spot them is by the fact that they endlessly call out their own name — 'chiffchaff, chiffchaff'! With the changing climate, some chiffchaffs now stay in Britain all year round and frost-free gardens on the south coast sometimes see these active little birds visiting even on the coldest days.

Bramble protection

Chiffchaffs are about the same size as a blue tit and are greenish-brown above and yellowish-white below. They spend most of their time up in trees and catching insects in mid air. They make their nests close to the ground, often in the middle of bramble patches to protect their eggs and chicks from **predators**.

male has a black cap

female has a
reddish-brown cap

Blackcap

Blackcaps are part of the warbler family and you can recognise the males by their jet-back 'cap'! However, females have a reddish-brown 'cap', and that can often confuse people into thinking they are two different types of bird. Blackcaps are one of the larger warblers and visit Britain from Spain, Portugal and Africa. Most blackcaps in this country are summer visitors but a small number of blackcaps now spend the winter here. These birds visiting in the colder months, come from Germany and other parts of northern Europe.

'Tack! Tack!'

Blackcaps often keep hidden in trees and bushes and are easiest to spot when they stop to deliver their beautiful song. When they are disturbed by humans or **predators** they give a loud, harsh warning call of 'tack', which is not such a lovely sound! Like chiffchaffs, blackcaps nest close to the ground. They feed their young on caterpillars, flies and other insects. Then, in late summer they start on the berries, as they fuel up in preparation for their long journey south.

Woodland Butterflies

Speckled Wood

Common in woods and gardens with plenty of trees, the speckled wood is currently spreading from its home in southern England, Wales and Ireland towards Scotland. Unlike many butterflies, the speckled wood prefers dappled shade. The males like to **bask**, only taking off to chase away a rival male or to persuade a female to stay and **mate**. You can see speckled woods in some gardens from April right through to October.

Look back to page 18 to remind yourself of a butterfly's lifecycle.

Brimstone

Brimstones are often the earliest butterflies to come out in the spring. The sight of a buttery-coloured male fluttering through your garden is a sign that spring has finally arrived. They **hibernate** in a tangle of ivy or a patch of brambles and, when they wake up, they are among the first insects to look for **nectar**. When they perch with their wings closed, their hooked shape and the pale green colour of the underside of their wings make them look just like a yellowing leaf.

Holly Blue

You are quite likely to spot a silvery blue male holly blue whizzing past, above head height, in the spring and summer, as they hunt down females. Holly blues like to wander, so you can even see them in the hearts of our towns and cities — in fact, anywhere with trees and bushes. In the spring, the females mostly lay their eggs on holly trees, but in the summer, they seem to prefer ivy instead. Both are common garden plants, so you are quite likely to see these butterflies in your garden.

Woodland Moths

The list of garden moths whose caterpillars feed on trees and shrubs is huge. These are some of the ones you are most likely to spot in your garden.

Creamy lines

December Moth

As you might guess from its name, this is one of very few moths out and about on Christmas Eve! Its hairy **abdomen** helps it keep warm on even the coldest nights. The female lays her eggs on tree leaves and, when the caterpillars hatch in spring, they only feed at night to avoid being spotted by hungry birds.

Charcoal-coloured wings

Common Marbled Carpet

Female common marbled carpet moths lay their eggs on woody plants like brambles, privet and hawthorn. This moth can be quite variable in colour, but the pattern on the wings always stays the same. Able to complete two whole life-cycles (or generations) in one year, this moth can be attracted to our gardens any time between May and early October.

Swallow Prominent

tuft of scales

You can recognise the moths in the prominent family by the tuft of scales they have on their wings, which sticks up when they're resting. Their caterpillars are bright green and feed on willow and poplar trees. In the south, this moth may have two life-cycles (or generations) in a year, flying from April to May and in August, but shorter summers in northern Britain mean that Scottish swallow prominents can only be found between July and September.

white, brown and black colouring

Peppered Moth

This moth can exist in two very different forms: one white with black 'peppering' and one black. You are more likely to see the light coloured form if you have a **rural** garden.

DID YOU KNOW?

The two forms of peppered moth **camouflage** with their surroundings. In areas with little or no pollution you usually see white peppered moths as they blend in perfectly with the **lichen** on trees. However, where there has been heavy pollution in the past, which would have killed the **lichen**, the black form is more common.

Big Beetles

cockchafer or May Bug

In the spring, you might see cockchafers attracted to any lights in your garden. These chunky beetles are also called May bugs. They are quite big, have brown wing-cases, a pair of amazing fanned **antennae** and a pointed bottom so it is not likely that you will confuse them with any other beetle! Their **larvae** feed on the roots of many garden plants, often chewing away underground for up to three years before changing into adult beetles. The adults like to feed on the leaves of apple trees, so some gardeners think they are a pest.

Stag Beetle

You are only likely to see a stag beetle in your garden if you live in southern England particularly the south east, and are lucky enough to have a lot of trees. The stag beetle is our largest and most impressive land beetle. The **larvae** feed on dead wood and it can take up to four years before they transform into adult beetles. The males can reach a length of eight centimetres. Their huge, pincer-like jaws might look scary but they only use them for fighting over females with other males.

Elm-Bark Beetle

You won't often see these beetles but you will see their terrible effects. These beetles are carriers of a deadly **fungus** which has wiped out elm trees right across Britain. Elm-bark beetles feed and **breed** on elm trees. The females lay their eggs in a tunnel just under the bark. When the eggs hatch and the **larvae** begin feeding, they create a pattern over the surface of the wood.

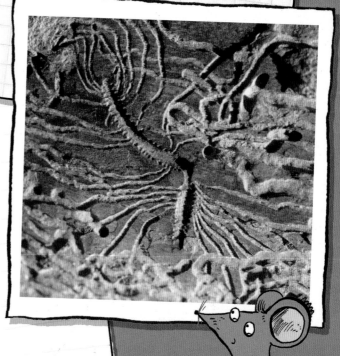

Welcoming Wildlife

Top Tips

1 If you have space, planting different types of tree will provide food for wildlife for most of the year. Self-sown seedlings are easy to plant and can save you money. If you ask permission from the landowner you might be able to take seedlings from waste ground or the countryside, or you could have fun trying to grow trees from seed.

2 Looking after your tree in its first few years of life will give it the best possible start. Supporting the tree with a stake, watering it if it is dry, protecting it from rabbits and squirrels and weeding around the base will all help the tree to establish itself in your garden.

3 Dense shrubs or mixed hedges are excellent places for birds to nest and for **mammals to hibernate**. They work particularly well along garden boundaries, working as barriers for humans but open borders for any wild visitors.

4 Don't forget that the woodland floor is an important **habitat**, too. Planting spring flowering plants will not only give you some cheerful early blooms but will also provide food for many insects as they wake up from **hibernation**.

5 Bird feeders give life-support to many birds in times of hardship. To keep your bird visitors healthy, it is important to clean the feeders regularly. Spacing them out around the garden will mean that more timid birds will get a chance to feed.

Wildlife-Friendly Plants

Ten great trees

Large
- Alder
- Ash
- Birch
- Oak
- Yew

Small
- Crabapple
- Hawthorn
- Hazel
- Holly
- Rowan

Five great woodland flowers
- English bluebell
- Daffodil
- Lesser celandine
- Lily of the valley
- Wood spurge

Ten great shrubs, bushes and climbers
- California lilac
- Mahonia
- Hebe
- Firethorn
- Wild privet
- Ivy
- Native honeysuckle
- Viburnum
- Wisteria
- Dog rose

Don't forget to keep digging up those worms for me!

Ponds

The single best way to make your garden more attractive to wildlife is to put in a pond. By doing this, you will encourage a whole variety of creatures into your garden that would normally pass by without a second glance. Ponds also provide hours of entertainment for you. Look out for dazzling dragonflies and love-struck frogs. And that's just above the water! Peer through the surface and some of the mini-beasts you'll see wouldn't be out of place in a horror film!

Ponds are home to animals like pond snails which spend their whole lives in water. There are also lots of animals like frogs, dragonflies and pond skaters which need water for an important part of their lifecycle. Finally, there are animals that don't actually live in water but are either attracted to food they find in it or just visit ponds for a drink or a bathe.

It doesn't matter if your garden isn't very big. Even the smallest container, sunk in the ground and kept topped up all year, will attract wildlife. It's amazing how quickly creatures will find your pond, flying, crawling or hopping in from far and wide. As many as half the ponds in the British countryside have been lost over the last century and many of the surviving ponds are in very poor condition. This means that garden ponds are now more important wildlife **sanctuaries** than ever.

The wetter the better!

Water-Loving Mammals

Otter

By the late 1970s, otters were nearly extinct in England because of pollution in rivers, the 'tidying up' of riverbank plants and hunting. However, since we have cleaned up our act and given the otter complete protection, it has surged back into our waterways.

PROTECTED

Shy and secretive

Over a metre long, with its tail included, the otter is just as happy on dry land as in water. Otters are shy and secretive so it is rare to see one. Often, the only sign an otter has visited you is its jasmine-scented poo on the banks of your pond! Otters never go far from streams and rivers but if you live nearby and have a pond with fish in it, then watch out!

American Mink

Much smaller than the otter, the dark-coloured American mink is an unwelcome visitor in the British countryside. Mink were brought here to be farmed for their fur but many escaped or were released and they have spread through our rivers and streams.

Otter helpers

Mink eat anything, from fish and birds, to voles and even chickens. They are ruthless killers. It can be hard to get rid of them but we have an unlikely helper. Otters and mink don't get on and, when they are both around, the bigger, stronger otter will send the mink packing!

Water Vole

Water voles are plump, with small ears, short tail and a 'doggy-paddle' swimming style. They live in burrows along riverbanks. Once a common sight in rivers, canals and ponds, they have become rarer in recent years. This is partly because of the disappearance of riverbank plants, which water voles need for food and shelter and also because of the spread of the American mink (which likes water vole for lunch). Mink are shy of people though, so water voles have found a haven in some rural gardens with large ponds.

Common Toad

Like their frog cousins, warty common toads have also found that gardens are the perfect place to **mate**, find food and **hibernate**. Toads have rougher skin than frogs and they also usually crawl or run, instead of hopping. If you look into a toad's eyes you will see that their pupils tend to be narrow, horizontal slits, whereas frogs have rounded pupils.

Those toads can't hop like us frogs!

Watch out for cars!

Toads wake up from **hibernation** over a few mild and wet evenings in early spring. They sometimes travel as far as several kilometres to reach their favourite ponds. Unfortunately, toads aren't aware how dangerous roads can be, so many are squashed by cars.

Fussy toads

Toads tend to be much fussier in their choice of pond than frogs. They prefer a pond to be large and fairly deep. When they **mate**, it can be noisy, with up to a dozen males fighting over a female. Frogspawn always forms in clumps but toadspawn is produced in long strings, just like pearls on a necklace. Whilst frog tadpoles are a favourite food for many pond **predators**, 'toadpoles' have poisonous skin which gives them some protection. By high summer, those that survive will have become 'toadlets' and be ready to crawl out of the pond on to dry land.

Night hunters

Gulp!

By May, once **mating** is over, adult toads leave the pond to find food. They hunt at night and will eat anything they can fit into their mouths such as ants, beetles, worms or slugs. The toad then hides under a stone or in a shallow burrow before the sun rises.

Newts

Smooth Newt

The smooth newt is the most common and widespread of the British newts. It is easiest to spot them from April, after they have arrived back at the pond for the **breeding season**. When he finds a female ready to **mate**, the male does an impressive underwater dance. Posing in front of her, he doubles his tail back on itself before quivering it in front of her nose! If the female is impressed, she will then allow him to **mate** with her. The females lay over 200 eggs, with each one carefully and individually laid on a different leaf.

long wavy crest

spotted body

orange belly

Baby newts

The young of these newts have feathery **gills** outside their bodies, which enable them to breathe underwater. They take three or four months to develop into adults so they don't leave the pond until late summer. They then stay on dry land during the autumn and winter, and return to the pond in spring to find a **mate**.

Palmate Newt

Palmate newts are the smallest of the British newts and you mainly see them in gardens close to upland or moorland. The males have flaps of skin (which are also called palmations) between the toes on their back feet, which they use to impress the females!

Hiding places

Adult palmate newts eat large numbers of frog tadpoles when they are in the pond but, once they leave the pond for dry land in July, they eat whatever they can catch! They spend up to eight months of the year out of water, so gardens with plenty of hiding places are very important for their survival.

long point at the end of the tail

Great-crested Newt

Great-crested newts are much bigger than the other British newts. They are found across lowland England and Wales and need plenty of hiding places close to their pond so that they can hunt for food and hide away. The numbers of great-crested newts have gone down so they are now protected by law and cannot be disturbed.

wavy crest along the tail

jagged crest along the back

black blotches make a different pattern on every newt

orange-yellow belly

Damselflies

Damselflies are smaller and more dainty than dragonflies. Another way to tell the difference is that damselflies lay their wings along the length of their bodies when they rest, rather than sticking them out to the sides.

Large Red Damselfly

Large red damselflies are usually the first of all the dragons and damsels to appear in the year – from as early as April. Large reds are the only red damselfly you'll see in your garden. They spend almost two years as **larvae** at the bottom of the pond, but the adults rarely live longer than a week. In their adult form they have just one thing to do before they die – **mate!**

Blue-tailed Damselfly

Look out for these damselflies between May and September. Blue-tailed damselfly **larvae** are very hardy and these damselflies can survive even in polluted ponds. The adults live for around a week. They like to eat smaller insects which they sometimes catch in mid-air.

black abdomen

brilliant blue segment

Azure Damselfly and common Blue Damselfly

Azure and common blue damselflies look very similar. The males of both kinds are a combination of blue and black. Azure damselflies tend to be found earlier in the year and the common blue in summer. When they **mate**, you might see them flying in pairs. The male holds the female just behind the head and hangs on tightly while she lays her eggs, to make sure no other males can interfere! When the eggs hatch, the **nymphs** feed like southern hawker dragonfly **larvae**, with a special 'mask'. They eat midge **larvae** and water fleas and grow quickly so they have to **shed** their skin up to ten times before they are ready to leave the water.

113

Water Snails

Water snails can't find your pond on their own; they have to be brought there. They often arrive stuck to the containers of pond plants! It is useful to have them in your pond as they keep the water clean by eating **algae** and dead plants. Their droppings also provide food for pond plants.

Great Pond Snail

The pointed shell of this large brown snail can reach around five centimetres in length. You might spot them at the surface of the water taking in air which they use to breathe underwater. During the summer, when there is plenty of food, they can build up extra layers of shell around the opening so that their shells become larger, giving them more space in which to grow.

Unlike most animals these snails aren't male or female but both! They lay their eggs in a sausage-shaped mass of jelly, underneath leaves at the surface of the water. The eggs hatch out into perfect miniature snails.

Great Ramshorn Snail

Great ramshorn snails get their name from their flat, coiled shells which look a bit like the horns of a male sheep (or ram). Their shells reach up to three centimetres across. Great ramshorns only eat plants so they like ponds with lots of the green stuff! They can live to three years of age. Like great pond snails they can be both male and female making it easier for them to fill an empty pond.

Pond Insects

Common Backswimmer

Common backswimmers can fly so they are usually one of the first insects to find new ponds. Look out for them hanging upside down from the surface of the water as they fill up their air supply. Backswimmers use their back legs to 'row' through the water as they chase down their **prey**.

Water Scorpion

Water scorpions use their front legs to grab other insects, tadpoles and even small fish. They aren't actually related to scorpions and don't have a sting. The long tube on their bottoms is actually used to suck air from above the water's surface.

Mayfly

Mayfly **nymphs** live for up to a year underwater, eating **algae** and plants. Look out for their three tails. If you disturb them underwater they will flick them quickly to escape. As adults, they live for less than a week. All the mayfly adults come out at once so that they can form a large **mating** swarm. Lots of different kinds of mayfly can be found in our ponds.

Caddisfly (Cinnamon sedge)

Caddisfly **larvae** build a case to hide in and to keep them safe. Different types build their cases out of different things: leaves, sand, or bits of rock. Cinnamon sedge **larvae** even use tiny pieces of stick! The **larvae** make silk to stick everything together. Adult caddisflies are most active in the evening and at night. You might see them fluttering around a light in your garden, like moths.

Great Diving Beetle

The **larvae** of this beetle are great hunters. They hang onto water plants and grab **prey** with their front legs. They then inject the **prey** with a special **substance** which turns its insides to liquid, so that they can then suck up the juices! The adult beetles reach three centimetres across and you might see them taking in air at the water's surface. This air is stored underneath their wing-cases. This air bubble makes the beetle much lighter than water – a bit like wearing armbands or a rubber ring when you are swimming – so they have to work very hard to dive to the bottom of the pond.

Alderfly

Most active at dusk, alderflies are not the strongest fliers so you might see them crawling around the water's edge or clinging to plants. The females lay their eggs near water so that the **larvae** drop off into the water when they hatch. The **larvae** spend the autumn and winter using their large, powerful jaws to catch any small pond creature that comes too near!

Common Pond Skater

Pond skaters are always one of the first creatures to find a new pond, as they can fly. You'll usually see them 'skating' jerkily over the surface of the water. They use their middle pair of legs to row like oars in a rowing boat, their back legs to steer and their shorter front legs to grab their **prey**. Any small insect which falls into the water creates ripples as it tries to break free of the surface. The pond skater senses these movements with hairs on its feet and then uses its **proboscis** to suck its **prey** dry.

The females lay their eggs in the spring, protecting them with a covering of jelly and sticking them to underwater plants. The young look just like small versions of the adults and **shed** their skin at least five times as they grow. They **hibernate** through the winter on dry land and then return to the pond as adults in the spring.

Whirligig Beetle

Look out for whirligig beetles in small 'schools', whizzing around the water surface. Whirligig beetles are the speed demons of the pond world and are small, glossy and black. Their middle and back pairs of legs are flattened into paddles, which helps them to skate so quickly.

Half and half

Whirligig beetles' eyes are divided into two, as they are specially made for a life on the surface of the water. The upper half is used for seeing in air, while the lower half is used to see underwater. If the beetle spots danger from above, it can dive down and hide in the plants underwater. Unlike the adults, the **larvae** spend all their time underwater where they feed on the **larvae** of midges and mosquitoes.

Welcoming Wildlife

Top Tips

1 Clean water is very important for a good wildlife pond. Try not to use tap water as it has chemicals in it which will make **algae** grow. Rainwater is best; if you are patient it will fill up your pond naturally. You could also use rainwater you have collected in a water butt.

2 A pond with lots of different depths will attract more different types of wildlife. Many pond creatures, like frogs, water beetles and dragonfly **larvae**, live mostly in shallow parts of the pond which are more easily warmed by the sun. Other creatures are helped by having deeper areas in ponds, which will not freeze solid in winter.

3 If you want a pond packed with wildlife, then don't keep fish in it. Fish are natural in many countryside ponds but they are top **predators** and can easily overwhelm a small garden pond. If you do want fish, why not dig a second pond just for them?

4 Try to grow lots of different water plants. This will make your pond more attractive to look at and more attractive to wildlife. Plants along the edge of the water give somewhere for dragonflies to perch and maybe even for birds to nest. Underwater plants add **oxygen** to the water and give pond mini-beasts somewhere to hunt and **breed**. Floating plants offer the perfect spot for newts, dragonflies and snails to lay their eggs.

5 Let the wildlife find your pond naturally. It is tempting to add some mud and pond water from an established pond to give it a kick-start but sometimes this can introduce diseases. In spring and summer, wildlife will quickly arrive without any help. Pond skaters, beetles and dragonflies will fly in and, with luck, frogs and newts will arrive too!

Ten great
pond wildlife plants

Frogbit

Hornwort

Marsh marigold

Bogbean

Spiked water milfoil

Water mint

Water-plantain

Water speedwell

Yellow flag iris

PROTECTED

Time to hop off!

Wild Areas, Compost Heaps and Log Piles

Areas where the grass has been left to grow, where wood has been left to rot or where dead plants haven't been tidied up are all really important spots for wildlife. In other words, a little bit of mess is good! Even in the tidiest of gardens there are corners which can't be used for much and these are important **sanctuaries** for many 'creepy-crawlies'.

To make your garden attractive to larger wildlife, you need as many of these creepy-crawlies as possible. You might not notice them, but insects, spiders and slugs are there in your garden in huge numbers, easily outnumbering your larger visitors and they have an important job to do. They are responsible for 'recycling' in your garden: removing waste and clearing up. They also act as food for larger animals.

The forgotten and unloved wild areas in your garden offer important **habitats** that animals might not be able to find elsewhere. Compost heaps are full of warm, rotting plants and provide the ideal place for slow worms and grass snakes to lay their eggs. The damp, dark conditions in a compost heap are also perfect for hundreds of different beetles, millipedes, centipedes and woodlice.

Piles of logs are ideal for wood-rotting mushrooms and toadstools and many beetles depend on dead wood to complete their life-cycle. These overgrown or forgotten corners are also often the best locations in the garden for birds to nest and for **mammals to hibernate** in the winter.

Mess is best!

Small Mammals

smaller eyes and ears than a mouse

blunt nose

shorter tail than a mouse

Bank Vole

Bank voles are a favourite food of tawny owls and foxes, so they try to spend most of their lives out of sight. They nest in underground burrows and move around in a network of 'covered' runways through long grass and shallow tunnels in the soil. In spring and summer they like to eat plant shoots and leaves; in autumn and winter they like mushrooms, berries and nuts. Bank voles have a lot of babies. They are able to **breed** from spring right through to autumn and females can produce up to five **litters** of three to five each year. That could be as many as 25 babies for each mother in a good year!

Common Shrew

Shrews mostly keep themselves well hidden and you are more likely to hear one than see one. They need to eat almost all the time to stay alive: insects, spiders, slugs, snails and woodlice all get gobbled up. Shrews rarely live much longer than a year and they don't like company. **Mating season** is the only time of year shrews spend together. They usually manage to have one or two **litters** of young during a year.

tiny, beady eyes

bristly whiskers

pointed snout

Brown Rat

Brown rats only arrived in Britain 300 years ago, as stowaways on ships, but they are now found everywhere! Rats are often associated with sewers and rubbish tips but you could well see one in your garden, too. They are able to eat more or less anything; eggs, frogs, nuts, berries and waste food all regularly appear on their menu.

Babies, babies, babies!

Rats often **breed** in a variety of warm and undisturbed places in the garden including compost bins. They can **breed** all year round. If the winter is mild, they could have over 50 young in a single year! The young themselves are able to **breed** after just a couple of months, so it's easy to see how rat numbers can skyrocket. Unfortunately, rats are able to pass diseases on to humans so this is one garden visitor we shouldn't welcome.

Lizards

Common Lizard

You are most likely to spot a common lizard warming itself on your wall or log-pile. They are found across large parts of Britain: anywhere there is a sunny garden with plenty of insects! Both males and females are brown with darker and lighter markings but the male's orange-red belly is very distinctive in the **breeding season.** Common lizards are slow moving when they are cold but, once warmed up, they become incredibly quick. They come out of **hibernation** in the spring and **mate.** The young are born in early summer and look just like tiny versions of their parents.

DID YOU KNOW?

Common lizards do get caught and eaten by cats, rats and birds but sometimes they can escape by the neat trick of losing their tail! With the **predator** distracted by the wriggling tail, the lizard quickly runs away.

Slow Worm

Slow worms are often mistaken for worms or small snakes but they are actually legless lizards. This makes it easy for them to hide or track down their **prey** in the smallest of places. Like all **reptiles**, slow worms need the sun's warmth to be active. They like to **bask** in the sun during the day, usually underneath a flat stone so that they can stay out of sight. Then, at night, they start tracking down slugs and snails.

Long life

Slow worms spend the coldest part of the year in **hibernation**. Males and females look quite similar and can vary in colour from light to dark brown. They **mate** in the spring and the females have between ten and twenty young in late summer. The young take around three years before they become adults. Cats, rats, foxes and hedgehogs all eat slow worms but those that manage to escape can live to a ripe, old age. One slow worm in **captivity** even managed to reach 50!

Grass Snake

Reaching over a metre in length, the grass snake is Britain's longest snake. In large English and Welsh gardens, you might spot one hunting around your pond or enjoying the warmth and shelter of your compost heap. They have a long, thin, olive green body, a yellow 'collar' around their necks and round, black eye pupils.

Compost heap nest

Like all British **reptiles**, grass snakes spend winter **hibernating**. They wake up and **mate** in the spring. The female builds a nest for her eggs; compost heaps and piles of dead leaves are favourite spots. She lays between 5 and 20 leathery eggs which don't hatch until August or September. The young look just like tiny, dark adults, and are independent from the start. They quickly slither away to find slugs and worms for themselves.

Frogs... yum!

Grass snakes are happiest in and around water and frogs are their favourite food, although they also eat small **mammals** and birds. The grass snake isn't venomous but it makes up for this with its backward curved teeth, which make it difficult for any **prey** to wriggle away. If a grass snake feels threatened it will hiss loudly and puff itself up to make it look bigger and more scary than it really is. If that doesn't work they can also make a foul-smelling liquid which puts other animals off, or, as a last resort, play dead.

Keep it away from me!

Beetles

Devil's Coach-Horse

These large beetles look pretty scary! If something frightens them, they can curl up their long **abdomens** to look like a menacing scorpion. This beetle's large head has a powerful pair of pincers, which can deliver a painful nip to any unwary human. It hides under logs or stones by day and comes out at night to catch anything smaller than itself!

Boo! Did I scare you?!

Rove Beetle

Rove beetles develop into adult beetles in the spring, and spend most of their time under stones or in compost heaps. They are red and black with a long abdomen and short wing cases. When they come out to feed, they use their speed to outrun smaller insects.

Sexton Beetle

Sexton beetles are also known as 'grave diggers'. They are important in recycling dead birds and **mammals** in your garden. They are attracted by the smell of rotting animals and they bury any dead body they find. They then lay their eggs on it. When the young hatch, they have a ready meal of rotting meat to eat!

Nettle Weevil

The nettle weevil is a small beetle with a brilliant golden-green or bluish-green colour that spends its whole life on or around nettles. You might spot the adults on any nettles in your garden in May or June, before they **mate** and die. The **larvae** then spend the rest of the year living in the soil, eating the nettle roots before they turn into adults the following spring.

Woodlice

Woodlice love the quiet corners of your garden. They are related to crabs and shrimps, which live in water, but woodlice live on land. They mainly come out at night and like dark, damp places, which help stop them from drying out.

Common Pygmy Woodlouse

The common pygmy woodlouse is tiny and reddish-brown in colour. They are the most common woodlouse in Britain. With seven pairs of legs and a narrow body, this woodlouse spends its entire life hiding in dead leaves or compost heaps. Like most woodlice, rotting plants are their favourite food.

Common Rough Woodlouse

Common rough woodlice grow up to two centimetres long and are slate-grey with a rough, pimply feel to their shells. These woodlice are better able to survive in dry conditions than many of their cousins. You can often find lots of them under bricks and stones or even behind loose bark on trees. If you disturb them they will quickly scuttle away.

Common Shiny Woodlouse

The common shiny woodlouse has a smooth, shiny body with light grey and yellow patches along the edges of its shell. These woodlice like to live in damp spots and use their **antennae** to find their way and to find food.

Common Pill Woodlouse

Dark grey in colour, this is the only woodlouse which can use its shell to roll up into a perfect, tight ball. This helps to protect them from being eaten and also stops them from drying out. Common pill woodlice are more common in gardens in south east England. They mostly eat rotting plants but they will also climb trees and walls to eat **lichen** and **algae**.

Welcoming Wildlife

Top Tips

1 Don't throw kitchen or garden waste away! It can all be turned into the most wonderful fertiliser to feed your flower beds. This will not just save you money at the garden centre but compost bins also provide food and **sanctuary** for a huge range of wildlife.

2 Making a log pile is a neat way to get rid of logs and makes the perfect home for many creatures. It is best to place the log pile somewhere shady and damp. Partly burying the bottom logs will speed up the rotting process. As the wood slowly rots down, keep the pile going by simply adding more to the top.

3 Try to leave quiet corners as undisturbed as possible. This is likely to be the spot where birds will attempt to **breed**. It will also give **sanctuary** to a number of creatures **hibernating** through the winter.

4 Some of the best plants for wildlife are those that the keen gardener might want to get rid of most. Weeds can sometimes overwhelm other plants if left unchecked, so why not choose a quiet corner where they can be left to run free? Any plants which spread too fast or too far, can simply be cut back.

5 Quiet corners do not have to be messy corners. A neat log-pile can look quite stylish and a compost heap can be like that kitchen cupboard that stores all the mess out of sight!

Wildlife-Friendly Plants

Ten great wildlife-friendly weeds

Bramble

Chickweed

Common groundsel

Fat hen

Garlic mustard

Grasses

Honesty

Nettle

Plantain

Above and Below

There are lots of garden animals that spend their lives hidden in the soil beneath our feet or flying around above our heads. Whether bats, swallows, house martins or swifts visit your garden depends a lot on where you live. If your garden is close to a spot where bats **roost** in the summer they are likely to come in to feed. Swifts nest mostly in town and city buildings, while swallows and house martins prefer a **rural** lifestyle.

Not everyone will be lucky enough to have bats or swallows visiting their garden but all garden soil is filled with a huge range of creatures. You wouldn't be able to see them without a microscope, but the soil is full of tiny plants and animals which release goodness into the soil for larger plants. The countless worms and springtails which live in the soil help to improve its structure and also act as food for everything from centipedes and moles to frogs and blackbirds.

Red Kite

Twenty years ago, red kites were one of Britain's rarest **birds of prey**, only surviving in a small area of central Wales. Luckily, scientists have managed to bring red kites back and you can see them across a wide area of the country. They are slightly larger than buzzards and are very graceful in flight. Look out for their long, reddish-coloured forked tail. When they fly, this tail is twitched from side to side as they adjust their position in the air.

Swooping in

Red kites **breed** in woodland and mostly eat dead animals. They also eat insects, worms and small **mammals**. In areas where there are lots of red kites they have been seen coming to gardens where meat scraps have been left out. They can swoop down and pick up food from the ground without needing to land.

Gulls

Herring Gull

Herring gulls look fierce with a permanent scowl, a light grey back and wings and a big, yellow beak with a hook at the tip. Their distinctive laughing call is an early alarm clock across many towns in Britain during the gull's **breeding season**. Herring gulls originally lived near the sea and it was only in the 1940s that they moved to towns and cities. They are attracted by the amount of food we leave lying around and there are now huge numbers **breeding** in some towns.

Feed us, feed us!

They like to nest close to other gulls on roofs and lay two to four eggs. They defend the area around the nest from **predators** - including humans! The chicks are **camouflaged** for the first few days after they hatch out, but after that, they move about more and hungrily mob their parents whenever they fly in with food.

Black-Headed Gull

In spring and summer, black-headed gulls are easy to recognise by their chocolate brown 'hoods'. In winter, their heads turn white with a brown spot on either side of their face, so their name isn't very accurate! They are Britain's smallest gulls and, unlike herring gulls, they don't **breed** in towns and cities. Instead, they nest in marshy places or on islands.

Lunch

They are drawn into towns to feed once the **breeding season** is over. In winter, look out for black-headed gulls early in the morning. They sometimes come to clear bird-tables of any leftovers. They don't often land in gardens; they swoop down for food before leaving to track down more lunch elsewhere.

Swallows, House Martins and Swifts

Swallow

Swallows spend their winters in South Africa so when they arrive back in Britain by early April, after an amazing 6,000-mile journey, it is a sign that spring is here. Swallows have a deeply forked tail and blue-black upper parts. They are paler underneath and have a reddish-brown face.

Watch out, insects!

Insect eaters

They like to nest in the roofs of old barns or sheds and don't like cities, so you are only likely to see them if you have a **rural** garden. They are very graceful birds and catch all of their food in mid air. They feed on flies, bugs and flying ants, and an adult swallow can catch as many as 6,000 insects a day to feed its chicks. They make open, cup-shaped nests out of mud and straw. In a good summer, they can have two or three **broods** of four or five chicks before they all begin the long journey back down south.

House Martin

House martins are another summer visitor to Britain. They are plumper and stockier than swallows and come to eat insects! Arriving in April, they stay in Britain until late October, if there are still lots of insects around. House martins like company and often nest alongside each other under the eaves of houses. They rebuild their cup-shaped nests from mud each year.

High fliers

When they are out feeding, house martins tend use the air space above swallows and you'll hear them twittering to one another. Martins use a fast, direct flight to catch enough gnats, flies and ants to keep their **brood** well fed. Even when the young have left the nest, their parents still feed them until they have got the hang of catching food for themselves.

Swift

With their short, torpedo-shaped bodies and curved wings, you can spot swifts by the 'anchor' shape they make in the sky. Even if you can't see them, you may be able to hear their screaming calls as they fly over your garden. Like swallows and house martins, swifts visit us for the summer and they are the last to arrive: they come in May and leave again in August.

Life in the air

They nest in the roof-spaces of buildings and when they aren't in the nest they spend all their time in the air: feeding, **mating** and even sleeping while flying! Swifts like company; look out for them chasing each other through the air. Any garden with plenty of trees and flowers is home to thousands of insects, which are the perfect food for these insect-eating machines. They only have one **brood** during the summer and from the moment the young take off, they may well not touch the ground again for two years until they return to **breed** as adults.

151

Moles

Many **mammals** come and go in your garden without being noticed but you will definitely notice if a mole moves in. Moles live underground so it is rare to see one, but their molehills on your lawn are hard to miss! Molehills are the leftover soil which the mole has dug out to make its underground network of tunnels and rooms.

Earthworms for lunch

Moles like to eat earthworms. The worms drop into the mole's tunnels and the mole picks them up as it goes along! Moles live alone and the only time they will consider company is during the short **mating season**. Baby moles are born in April or May and are naked, blind and helpless at first. It only takes six weeks for them to be ready to go off and find a garden of their own, though!

Many gardeners hate moles because they make a mess, but they do improve the soil by allowing air in. They also eat lots of pests like cockchafer **larvae** and leatherjackets.

Time to go underground!

Life underground

The mole is perfectly designed for life underground. They are covered in dense, velvety fur and their shape means that they are able to go backwards and forwards along their tunnels. Moles are small but they are surprisingly strong and can easily dig through the soil with their shovel-like arms.

Underground Minibeasts

Earthworms are some of the most important creatures in your garden. They help to break down rotting leaves and improve the structure of soil as they burrow through it. They also act as food for many other visitors to your garden.

Lob Worm

Lob worms can reach up to 35 centimetres long. They are the largest garden worm and the one you are most likely to see. Their head and tail ends are both pointed and they have a raised 'saddle' in the middle. They are purplish-brown in colour and have small bristles along their bodies which help them to grip when they move through the soil.

Deep burrows

Lob worms create deep burrows in the soil. They come up to the surface to feed, pulling leaves into their burrows which they store to eat later. Lob worms also come to the surface when they are **mating**, which they usually do on damp evenings after dark. Badgers, foxes and hedgehogs all like to eat them though, so they have to stay close to their escape burrows!

Black-Headed Worm

Black-headed worms can grow to about 15 centimetres long and are long and thin. Their heads are much darker in colour than their tails. They are most active when the soil is damp. In very dry weather they rest, curling up into a ball to save water. They live in burrows which can be as deep as 60 centimetres and, unlike lob worms, they **mate** underground, out of sight of hungry **predators**.

Did you know?

Black-headed worms are the ones who make 'worm casts' on your lawn in spring and autumn. These worm casts are actually the black-headed worm's poo!

Springtails

There can be thousands of springtails in a small patch of dead leaves, so imagine how many there must be in your whole garden! They are only about four millimetres in length so you'll only just be able to see them.

They like to live anywhere in your garden where it is damp, dark and wet. They have a forked, tail-like body part, which they can flick if they are disturbed, firing themselves into the air and out of harm's way. Springtails are very important in your garden as they eat dead plants and leaves and recycle the goodness.

Welcoming Wildlife

Top Tips

1 The key to making your garden attractive to flying insect-eaters is making your garden home to all manner of flying insects! Planting flowers, and lots of them, will attract these insects to your garden.

2 Remember, your garden is only as good as what is below it! Adding your own compost to the soil will boost the number of tiny plants and animals, earthworms, millipedes and woodlice living there. Compost will not only mean your flowers and vegetables do better, but will also make your garden much more inviting for wildlife: a 'win win' situation!

Wildlife Words

Abdomen (Abdomens) back part of an insect or spider's body

Algae plant with no roots, stems or leaves that grows in water

Amphibians cold-blooded animals that live both in water and on land but lay their eggs in water

Antennae long, thin feelers on the heads of insects

Bask (Basking) lie in the heat of the sun

Bird of prey bird that hunts and feeds on other animals

Breast front part of a bird's body, below its neck

Breed mate and then produce young

Breeding season time of the year when animals come together to breed

Brood (Broods) family of young animals born at the same time

Camouflage (Camouflaged) colours and patterns on an animal to help it hide or blend in with its surroundings

Canopy highest parts of trees, made up of branches and twigs and leaves

Captivity animals being kept somewhere by humans, such as in a zoo or as a pet

Chrysalis hard case formed by a moth or butterfly larva in which it lives while it is turning into an adult

Cocoon silky case spun by a larva to protect itself while it is turning into an adult

Conifer evergreen tree that has needle-like leaves and cones

Crest tuft of feathers, fur or skin on an animal's head

Descendants all the offspring from previous generations of animals

Evolved gradually changed over a long period of time

Eyespot marking that looks like an eye

Forewings the two front wings of an insect that has four wings

Fungus type of living thing that is not a plant or an animal, and lives on dead or decaying things

Gills part of the body which fish use to breathe underwater

Habitat (Habitats) natural home of an animal

Hibernate (Hibernation) spend the winter in a deep sleep

Hind back part of an animal or insect

Intruders people or animals who come in when they are not welcome

Larva (Larvae) baby insect

Lichen simple plant that grows on rocks, walls and trees

Litters families of baby animals born at the same time

Mammal (Mammals) warm-blooded animals that have hair or fur, give birth to live babies and feed them with their own milk

Mate (Mating) when two animals come together to breed

Mating season time of the year when animals come together to mate

Mature adult, grown-up

Native coming from a particular place, rather than being taken there or arriving there later

Nectar sugary liquid inside flowers that is collected by a variety of insects for food

Nymphs baby insects

Oxygen gas in the air, which humans and animals need to breathe

Paralyse make unable to move

Pollen a fine dust in plants that is carried from one plant to another so that the plants can produce seeds and fruit

Pollinate (Pollinates) carry pollen from one plant to another, to allow plants to produce fruit and seeds

Predator (Predators) animals that hunt and kill other animals for food

Prey animals that are hunted and killed by other animals for food

Proboscis long flexible mouth tube used for sucking

Rear back

Reptiles cold-blooded animals that have dry, scaly skin and lay eggs on land

Roost settle down to rest or sleep

Rural in the countryside

Sanctuary safe place

Scientific evidence something that has been proved by a science study or experiment

Shed lose skin

Substance material from which something is made

Territory area of land where an animal lives, defending it from other animals

Thorax middle body part of an insect or spider

Urban in a town or city

Venom poison injected into another animal by stinging or biting

Index

alderfly 118
American mink 103

badger 10, 52–53
bat 139, 140–141
bee 28–31, 33–35
bee-fly 40
bird of prey 70–71, 142–145
blackbird 14, 48, 71, 139
blackcap 89
blue tit 47, 80, 88
bluebottle 41
brambling 87
bullfinch 85
bumblebee 7, 28–29
butterfly 7, 18–22, 48, 90–91
buzzard 13, 142, 143, 144

caddisfly 117
centipede 123, 134–135, 139
chaffinch 82, 87
chiffchaff 88, 89
coal tit 81
cockchafer 96, 152
collared dove 69
common backswimmer 116
common flower bug 36
common froghopper 37
crane-fly 40

damselfly 112–113
deer 58–61
devil's coach-horse 130

dragonfly 101, 110–112, 120
dunnock 66

earthworm 14,15, 53, 64, 154–155
earwig 46
elm-bark beetle 97

fieldfare 79
fox 8–9, 13, 127
frog 101, 104–105, 120, 129, 139

goldcrest 67
goldfinch 84
gooseberry sawfly 41
grass snake 123, 128–129
great diving beetle 117
great tit 80, 94
green lacewing 47
greenfinch 83, 86
greenfly 36, 38,39, 41, 47
gull 146–147

hare 12
harvestman 45
hedgehog 7, 10–11, 48, 127
hornet 32
house martin 139, 150
house sparrow 66

jackdaw 75
jay 75

ladybird 38–39
leatherjacket 40, 152
lily beetle 39
lizard 126–127
long-tailed tit 81

magpie 74
marmalade hoverfly 41
mayfly 116
millipede 123, 134–135
mink 103
mole 139, 152–153
moth 23–27, 48, 92–95
mouse 62–63

nettle weevil 131
newt 108–109, 120
nuthatch 76
nymph 37, 46, 113

otter 102–103

pied wagtail 17
pigeon 68–69
pond skater 101, 118, 120

rabbit 12–13
rat 71, 125, 127
red kite 144–145
redwing 78, 79
robin 64
rove beetle 130

Saint Mark's fly 40
sexton beetle 131

shrew 124
siskin 86
slow worm 123, 127
slug 10, 42–43, 48, 105, 107, 123,124, 127, 129
snail 15, 42–43, 105, 114–115, 120, 124, 127
sparrowhawk 70
spider 44–45, 48, 51, 64, 67, 76,77, 123,124
springtail 155
squirrel 54–57, 71
stag beetle 97
starling 16, 71
swallow 139, 148–151
swift 139, 151

tadpole 104–105, 107–109, 111
tawny owl 71
thrush family 14–15, 48
toad 106–107
treecreeper 77

violet ground beetle 39
vole 103, 124

wasp 30–32
water scorpion 116
waxwing 79
whirligig beetle 119
woodlouse 123,124, 132–133
woodpecker 72–73
wren 65